Contents

Pearson Education Limited
Edinburgh Gate
Harlow
Essex CM20 2JE
England
and Associated Companies throughout the world.

Poptropica® English Islands

Editorial and project management by hyphen

First published 2017

Eighth impression 2022

ISBN: 978-1-2921-9809-5

Set in Fiendstar 17/21pt
Printed in Neografia, Slovakia

Acknowledgements: The publisher would like to thank Tessa Lochowski, Steve Elsworth and Jim Rose for their contributions to this edition.

Illustrators: Adam Clay, Leo Cultura, Joelle Dreidemy (Bright Agency), Tom Heard (Bright Agency), Andrew Hennessey, Marek Jagucki, Sue King, Stephanine Lau, Daniel Limon (Beehive Illustration), Katie McDee, Bill Mcguire (Shannon Associates), Jim Peacock (Beehive Illustration), Baz Rowell (Beehive Illustration), Jackie Stafford, Olimpia Wong, Teddy Wong and Yam Wai Lun

Picture Credits:
The publisher would like to thank the following for their kind permission to reproduce their photographs:

(Key: b-bottom; c-centre; l-left; r-right; t-top)

123RF.com: 86tc/3, 90c/5, 94tl, Anyka 14l/2, 20cr (d), Frank Bach 62bc, Belchonock 19c/2, Marie-Ann Daloia 62br, Gekaskr 96c (b), Roger Hall 73br, Nytumbleweeds 40cr, Paffy 85c, Pat138241 42br, Marina Scurupii 40br/4, Strelok 86c/9, Sirikorn Thamniyom 85b, Leah-Anne Thompson 90tc/2, Eleonora Vatel 81bl (a), Tracy Whiteside 43b; **Alamy Images:** Paul Brown 51cr, Design Pics Inc 95cr, Hero Images Inc. 29c, Alistair Laming 72tr, Eddie Linssen 51tr, MITO images 84tl, YAY Media AS 14c/4, 20cl (e); **Brand X Pictures:** Burke Triolo Productions 84bc/7, Burke Triolo Productions. 81cr (Fruit), 86tc/2; **Comstock Images:** 68cr/8; **Datacraft Co Ltd:** 72br (a); **Digital Vision:** 62bl; **Fotolia. com:** 2xSamara.com 19cr/4, Asbtkb 64cl, BestPhotoStudio 84tr, Ruth Black 19cl/1, Sergiy Bykhunenko 84tc, Jacek Chabraszewski 14l/1, 14c/5, 20c (f), 20cl (a), Viktor Chinkoff 64tl, Coloures-pic 42bl, Antonio Diaz 30br, D. Fabri 62cr, Sergii Figurnyi 63bc (Mouse), Elisabetta Figus 90tl/1, Fivespots 63bl (Snake), Vadim Gnidash 18tc/2, Marina Ignatova 94cr/4, 94bl (a), JackF 41cl, Jonnysek 63br (Rabbit), Lana Langlois 63bc (Lizard), Markus Mainka 31br, Pixel Memoirs 63cl, Monkey Business 42c (Tractor), Piotr Pawinski 68tc/2, SergiyN 10tc/3, 21bc, 30bl, 74bl, Soleg 40tc, Star Jumper 18bl/4, Stockphoto-Graf 80 (Ice Cream), Leah-Anne Thompson 14cl/3, 20c (g), Scott Waby 63bl (Tarantula), WavebreakMediaMicro 29cr, Werg 63c, Ivonne Wierink 19c/3, Womue 80 (Fruit), 84br/8, YellowCrest 73cr; **Getty Images:** Digital Vision. 28cr, FotografiaBasica 40tr, SA2RN 84cl, Sadeugra 40c, VvoeVale 40bl/1, Yuri 69c; **Pearson Education Ltd:** Studio 8 29cl, 90cr/7, Trevor Clifford 10tl/1, 10tc/2, 10tr/4, 10c/6, 10cl/5, 10cr/7, 10cr/8, 50tl, 50tr, 50cl, 50cr, 52tc, 63tl, 63tr, 104cr, 104br, 105cr, 105br, 106cr, 106br, Jules Selmes 14r/7, 20cr (h), Rafal Trubisz, Marcin Rosinski. Pearson Central Europe SP. Z.O.O. 14cr/6, 20c (b); **PhotoDisc:** Tony Gable. C Squared Studios. 28tc (Drum); **Shutterstock. com:** 3445128471 15bl, 96bl, 18c/2 (Fish), 96cl (a), AMC Photography 81bl (c), Petrenko Andriy 20bl, Venus Angel 68tl/1, Apollofoto 47cr, Artcasta 86tc/4, Tom Asz 72cr, AVAVA 29tr, Baloncici 68tc/3, Beata Becla 74tl, Mark Bonham 55t, Butterfly Hunter 18c/5 (Butterfly), Kenneth William Caleno 86c/8, Cheryl Casey 90tr/3, Massimo Cattaneo 62tl, Jacek Chabraszewski 52br, Steven Chiang 28bl, Lucian Coman 94c/2, 94bc (c), Corepics VOF 72br (b), Couperfield 84bc/3, Cre8tive Images 80 (Chocolate), CreativeNature.nl. 64c, Digital Media Pro 63tc, Elena Efimova 64cr, Ene 81bl (b), Slawomir Fajer 90c/6, Fotocraft 74cl, Fotomak 94tr, FrameAngel. 68c/6, Terri Francis 72tl, Filip Fuxa 72cl, Gelpi 25bc, 96br, Deyan Georgiev 96cr (d), Volodymyr Goinyk 94tc, Joe Gough 80 (Meat), Ramona Heim 95cl, Brent Hofacker 86cr/10, Hwongcc 18tr/3, Iko 19tr, Italianestro. 28tr, Jackhollingsworth.com 85t, Matt Jeppson 64tr, jirasaki 15br, Junial Enterprises 25br, Kamira 84cr, Karamysh 74cr, Melissa King 95r, Dmitriy Krasko 81cr (Meat), 84br/4, Stephen Lew 94cl/1, 94bc (b), Lizard 81cl (Bowl), Veronica Louro 74br, Lubava 62c, M.bonotto 51br, Cosmin Manci 18cr/3, Mau Horng 80 (Cake), 86cl/6, Nataliia Melnychuk 64tc, Mexrix 80 (Yogurt), 84bl/5, 86c/7, MishAl 68tr/4, Monkey Business Images 41c, 73cl, 73bl, Monticello 81c (Bread), Mylisa 80 (Cheese), 84bc/2, Olga Nayashkova 86tr/5, Nbriam 18c/4 (Leaf), Neamov. 28tc (Piano), Nejron Photo 42c (Dentist), Newphotoservice 72tc, Tomasz Nieweglowski 40bc/3, Nito 80 (Jelly), Odua Images 42cl, Alena Ozerova 14cr/8, 20c (c), Siamionau Pavel 84bl/1, Preto Perola 84bc/6, Pictures_ for_You 40bc/2, pr2is 94c/3, 94br (d), Inara Prusakova 40tl, Yevgen Romanenko 81c (Cheese), Romrodphoto 95l, Room27 68cl/5, Rossario 72br (c), Dario Sabljak 28tl, Pablo Scapinachis 74tc, SergiyN 31bl, 53bl, Serp. 18br/5, Anastasia Shilova 64bl, Artazum and Iriana Shiyan 74tr, Shyamalamuralinath 52bl, 73tl, Sixninepixels 68c/7, Ljupco Smokovski 80 (Honey), Syda Productions 90cl/4, TijanaM 64br, Solomiya Trylovska 28br, Tsekhmister 81bl (d), TTstudio 18cl/1 (Daffodil), Tupungato 73tr, Urfin 62cl, Vishnevskiy Vasily 18tl/1, 62tr, Volkova 63cr, Wavebreakmedia. 28cl, Monika Wisniewska 42cr, Anke van Wyk 62tc, Zurbagan 86tl/1; **SuperStock:** Ingram Publishing. Alamy 96c (c)

Cover images: *Back:* **Fotolia.com:** frender r; **Shutterstock.com:** Denys Prykhodov l

Welcome

Vocabulary:	**Colours:** blue, green, red, yellow **Numbers:** one, two, three, four, five, six, seven, eight, nine, ten **Classroom actions:** stand up, sit down, look, listen, count, open your book, close your book, wave goodbye
Structures:	Hello. I'm (Harry). My name's (Harry). Goodbye. His/Her name's (Harry). His/Her (balloon) is red.

1 My birthday

Vocabulary:	**Colours:** pink, purple, orange, brown, black, white, grey **Actions:** clap, stamp, jump, walk, run, dance, hop, climb **Natural science:** bird, fish, flower, leaf, butterfly		**Values:** It's good to share. **Phonics:** a, p, s, t (at, pat, sat, tap) **CLIL:** Natural science (Colours in nature) **Wider World:** A birthday party
Structures:	What's your name? My name's (Cody). How old are you? I'm (seven). What's your favourite colour? My favourite colour is (green).	Is it (purple)? Yes, it is./No, it isn't. What colour is it? It's (pink).	

2 At school

Vocabulary:	**Classroom objects:** book, pen, pencil, ruler, rubber, pencil sharpener, pencil case, table, chair, desk **Numbers:** eleven, twelve, thirteen, fourteen, fifteen, sixteen, seventeen, eighteen, nineteen, twenty **Music:** violin, drum, guitar, piano		**Values:** Try hard at school. **Phonics:** d, i, m, n (dip, dad, it, sit, man, am, nap, pan) **CLIL:** Music (Musical instruments) **Wider World:** My school
Structures:	What's this? It's a (book). It's red. It's a (red) (book).	What are these? They're (pencils). What colour are they? They're (red). How many (pencils) can you see? (Five).	

3 My family

Vocabulary:	**Family members:** mum, dad, brother, sister, granny, grandad, friend, aunt **Occupations:** vet, pilot, doctor, dancer, cook, farmer, dentist, artist, teacher **Art:** painting, collage, sculpture, drawing		**Values:** Love your family. **Phonics:** c, g, o (can, cap, cat, gas, dig, on, dog, top) **CLIL:** Art (Types of art) **Wider World:** Different families
Structures:	This is my brother/sister. How old is he/she? He's/She's (nine).	Is he/she a (vet)? Yes, he/she is. Is he/she an (artist)? No, he/she isn't. He's/She's a (teacher).	

4 My body

Vocabulary:	**Parts of the body:** body, head, arms, hands, fingers, legs, feet, toes, tail, wings **Clothes:** T-shirt, jumper, trousers, dress, skirt, shoes, socks, hat **Natural science:** a dirty face, clean hands, dirty hands, wash your hands		**Values:** Be clean. **Phonics:** ck, e, k (kick, sock, pen, pet, ten, neck, kid, kit) **CLIL:** Natural science (Personal hygiene) **Wider World:** Carnivals in the UK
Structures:	I've got a (green) (tail). I've got (green) (arms).	He's/She's got a (red) (hat). He's/She's got (blue) (trousers). He's/She's got (one) (head). It's (yellow). He's/She's got (four) (legs). They're (purple).	

5 Pets

Vocabulary:	Pets: dog, cat, rabbit, mouse, tortoise, parrot, frog, snake, hamster Adjectives: big, small, tall, short, long, thin, fat, young, old Natural science: bird, chick, kitten, puppy, goose, egg
Structures:	What's that? It's a (dog). What are those? They're (hamsters). Have you got a (parrot)? Yes, I have. It's a (small) (parrot)./No, I haven't. Has he/she got a (parrot)? Yes, he/she has. It's a (small) (parrot)./ No, he/she hasn't. He's/She's got a (big) (dog).

Values: Take care of your pets.
Phonics: b, h, r, u
(bag, rug, hot, hat, red, rat, up, cup)
CLIL: Natural science
(Baby animals)
Wider World: Unusual pets

6 My house

Vocabulary:	At home (1): house, living room, kitchen, bedroom, bathroom, garden, window, door At home (2): bed, cooker, fridge, TV, sofa, lamp, bath, sink Social science: shop, library, playground, park, café
Structures:	Where's (Aunt Fifi)? She's in the (living room). Where are (Waldo and Beth)? They're in the (bedroom). There's a (lamp) on the (desk). There are (two kittens) under the (sofa).

Values: Be tidy.
Phonics: f, ff, l, ll
(fig, fan, off, puff, leg, lap, doll, bell)
CLIL: Social science (Public places)
Wider World: Different homes

7 Food

Vocabulary:	Food (1): fruit, cheese, bread, cake, salad, milk, juice, yoghurt, fish Food (2): sandwich, water, chocolate, honey, jelly, vegetables, ice cream, meat Natural science: sausages, carrots, chips	
Structures:	I like (cake) and (milk). I don't like (salad) and (fish).	Do you like (honey)? Yes, I do./No, I don't.

Values: Be polite.
Phonics: j, ss, v, w
(jam, jet, kiss, mess, van, vet, web, wig)
CLIL: Natural science
(Healthy eating)
Wider World: Packed lunches

8 I'm happy!

Vocabulary:	Adjectives (1): tired, hungry, thirsty, scared, happy Adjectives (2): sad, cold, hot, ill, hurt, angry, bored Social science: It's hot. It's cold.
Structures:	Are you (hungry)? Yes, I am./No, I'm not. Is he/she (cold)? Yes, he/she is./No, he/she isn't. He's/She's (hurt). Are they (bored)? Yes, they are./No, they aren't. They're (tired).

Values: Respect feelings. Help others.
Phonics: qu, x, y, z, zz
(quiz, quick, box, taxi, yes, yell, zap, zip, buzz, fizz)
CLIL: Social science (Hot and cold places)
Wider World: Hot and cold places in the USA

Goodbye

Vocabulary:	Quest items: balloon, cake, tablet, photo, teddy, bird, door, apple, hat	
Structures:	Where's the (balloon)? I've got the (photo). There's a (bird).	How many (sandwiches) can you see? Has he got a (parrot)? Has she got (blue shoes)? Where's (the frog)? Is he (happy)?

Festivals

Halloween: witch, monster, cat, bat, pumpkin
Christmas: Santa, reindeer, sleigh, present
Easter: egg, bunny, chick
Summer fun: sun, sky, tree, flower, bird, grass

Welcome

Hello. My name's Waldo.

1 1:02 Listen and trace. Then say.

Hello. I'm Harry.

Waldo

Beth

Harry

2 1:03 Listen and find.

3 Point and say.

4 1:04 Listen and chant.

Beth.

Blue.

a blue

b green

c red

d yellow

See the colours of the flowers.
Red, red flowers. Yellow, yellow flowers.
Colours, colours, everywhere.
Blue, blue flowers. Green, green flowers.
Colours, colours, everywhere.

Can identify colours

1:05

Hello.	I'm Harry.
	My name's Harry.
Goodbye.	

I'm = I am   name's = name is

Cody

Aunt Fifi

5 **Listen and circle. Then say.** 1:06

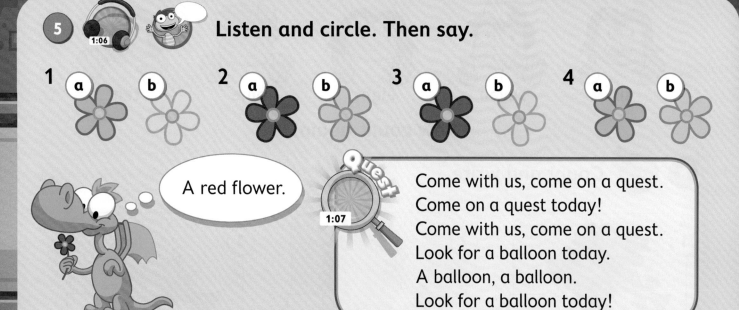

1 a b   2 a b   3 a b   4 a b

A red flower.

Quest 1:07

Come with us, come on a quest.
Come on a quest today!
Come with us, come on a quest.
Look for a balloon today.
A balloon, a balloon.
Look for a balloon today!

 **6** **Listen and point. Then listen again and say.**

one   two   three   four   five

six   seven   eight   nine   ten

7 **Listen, count and chant.**

one   two   three   four   five

six   seven   eight   nine   ten

Now count again!

8 **Count and write.**

  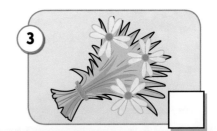

1   2   3

 **9**   **Listen and match. Then say.**

1:12

1:11

His name's Harry.
His balloon is red.

Her name's Beth.
Her balloon is blue.

1 **Harry**

2 **Cody**

3 **Beth**

4 **Waldo**

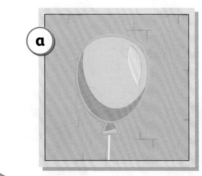
a

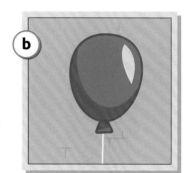
b

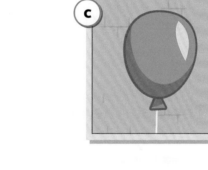
c

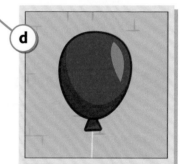
d

Number 1!

His name's Harry.
His balloon is red.

 10   **Draw a classmate and guess.**

Her name's Ana.
Her balloon is yellow.

11  **Listen and do the actions. Then listen again and say.**

①
stand up

②
sit down

③
look

④
listen

⑤
count

⑥
open your book

⑦
close your book

⑧
wave goodbye

12  **Listen and chant. Then do the actions.**

Stand up, sit down,
And listen to me.
Open your book
And count to three!

Sit down, stand up,
And look at me.
Close your book
And wave goodbye!

Can identify classroom actions

13   **Listen and point. Then play the game.**

1 My birthday

1 **What do you know?**

2  **Listen.**

pink

purple

orange

brown

3   **Listen and circle.**

4   **Listen and say.**

5  **Listen and chant.**

Name, name. What's your name?
Beth, Beth. My name's Beth.

Age, age. How old are you?
Six, six. I'm six.

Colour, colour. What's your favourite colour?
Blue, blue. My favourite colour is blue.

Can identify more colours

LOOK!

1:21

What's your name?	**My name's** Cody.
How old are you?	**I'm** seven.
What's your favourite colour?	**My favourite colour is** green.

What's = What is

black

white

grey

6 1:22 **Listen and write.
Then ask and answer.**

1:23 Quest

Look for a cake today.
A balloon and a cake!
Look for a cake today!

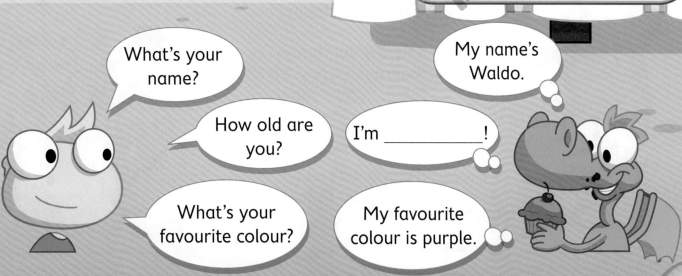

What's your
name?

My name's
Waldo.

How old are
you?

I'm _____!

What's your
favourite colour?

My favourite
colour is purple.

7 1:25 Listen and do the actions.
Then listen again and say.

①  ②  ③  ④  ⑤  ⑥  ⑦  ⑧

clap   stamp   jump   walk   run   dance   hop   climb

8  1:26 Listen. Then sing and do the actions.

Happy Birthday!

It's my birthday!
Hip hip hurray! Happy birthday!
Clap, clap, clap.

I'm six today!

It's my birthday!
Hip hip hurray! Happy birthday!
Stamp, stamp, stamp.

I'm seven today!

It's my birthday!
Hip hip hurray! Happy birthday!
Jump, jump, jump.

I'm eight today.

Happy birthday!
Happy birthday!

Cut-outs
p:113

9 **Listen and stick.**

 **LOOK!**

Is it purple?	Yes, **it is**.
	No, **it isn't**.
What colour is it?	**It's** pink.

isn't = is not   It's = It is

1

1

2

3

4

10 **Look and play.**

1

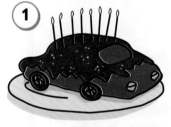

2

3

4

Is it red?

Number 1!

Yes, it is.

 It's good to share.

12 Listen.

① **a** ② **p** ③ **s** ④ **t**

13   Listen, point and say.

14   Listen and blend the sounds.

1 a – t   at

2 p – a – t   pat

3 s – a – t   sat

4 t – a – p   tap

15 Underline *a*, *p* and *t*. Read the words aloud.

1 pat

2 tap

16 **Listen and point. Then say.**

1 bird

2 fish

3 flower

4 leaf

5 butterfly

17   **Complete the pictures. Then say.**

1

2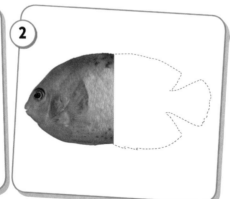

3

What colour is it?

It's yellow.

A flower!

4

5

Wider World

A birthday party

  18 1:38 **Listen and read. Then trace.**

Hello. My name's Kim. It's my birthday today!

1

Look at my birthday cake! I'm seven.

2

Look at my balloons. My favourite colours are pink and purple.

3

One, two, three, four, five, six presents!

4

Happy birthday to me.

19 **Read and match. Then say.**

1   My name's   seven.

2   I'm   Kim.

3   Happy   birthday to me.

20 **PROJECT**

1 **Draw** your birthday party.
2 **Write** about your picture.
3 **Talk** about your picture with your classmates.

Talk to your family about their birthdays.

21 🎧 1:39 ✏️ **Listen and ✓.**

1

2

3

4

⭐

22 🎧 1:40 ✏️ **Listen and number.**

a

b

c

d

e

f

g

h

⭐

23 ✏️ 😀 **Write. Then ask and answer.**

What's your name?

How old are you?

What's your favourite colour?

My name's _____.

I'm _____.

My favourite colour is _____.

⭐

I CAN DO IT!

Can assess what I have learnt in Unit 1

24 **Find, count and write.**

①
cake

②
balloon

③
butterfly

④
flower

⑤
flower

⑥
bird

25 **Find and say.**

Three red balloons.

2 At school

1 ⭐ **What do you know?**

2 🎧 1:41 **Listen.**

chair

desk

ruler

pencil case

pencil

pencil sharpener

table

A yellow pencil and a
blue pen.
A pink pencil case and an
orange pencil sharpener.
A green ruler and a
white rubber.
A purple book.
Look, look, look!

3  **Listen and circle.**

4  **Listen and say.**

5 **Listen and chant.**

Can identify classroom objects

1 2 3 4 5

1:45

LOOK!

What's this? | It's a book. It's red.
It's a red book.

book

rubber

pen

6 **1:46** Listen and number. Then ask and answer.

a

b

c

d

What's this?

It's a yellow pen.

Quest **1:47** Look for a tablet today.
A balloon, a cake and a tablet!
Look for a tablet today!

7   **Listen and stick.**
Then listen again and say.

eleven   twelve   thirteen   fourteen   fifteen

Stick

sixteen   seventeen   eighteen   nineteen   twenty

8  **Listen, count and write the numbers.**
Then sing.

SONG

Rulers, rulers. How many rulers?
How many rulers can you see?
Hurray! Let's play.
Let's jump and climb. **11**

Books, books. How many books?
How many books can you see?
Hurray! Let's play.
Let's jump and climb. ☐

Pencils, pencils. How many pencils?
How many pencils can you see?
Hurray! Let's play.
Let's jump and climb. ☐

TIP!

one ruler /
two rulers

Pens, pens. How many pens?
How many pens can you see?
Hurray! Let's play.
Let's jump and climb. ☐

Rubbers, rubbers. How many rubbers?
How many rubbers can you see?
Hurray! Let's play.
Let's jump and climb. ☐

Cut-outs

p:115

LOOK! 1:51

What are these?	They're pencils.
What colour are they?	They're red.
How many pencils can you see?	Five.
They're = They are	

How many chairs can you see?

Two.

9 1:52 **Listen and circle. Then ask and answer.**

1 a  b

2 a 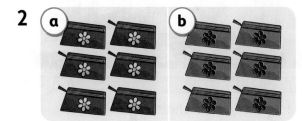 b

3 a 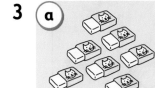 b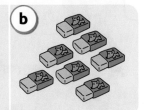

4 a  b

10 **Draw. Then ask and answer.**

 SKILLS

1

2

What are these?

They're pencils.

What colour are they?

They're green.

Listen and read. Then act out.

 Try hard at school.

Can understand and act out a simple story

12  Listen.

① **d** ② **i** ③ **m** ④ **n**

13  Listen, point and say.

14 Listen and blend the sounds.

1 d - i - p dip   2 d - a - d dad

3 i - t it   4 s - i - t sit

5 m - a - n man   6 a - m am

7 n - a - p nap   8 p - a - n pan

15 Underline *d*, *i*, *m* and *n*. Read the words aloud.

1 man   2 dip   3 nap

4 pan   5 sit   6 dad

16 🎧 1:62 😀 **Listen and number. Then say.**

a

b

drum ☐

c

d

violin ☐

piano ☐

guitar ☐

MUSIC

17 🎧 1:63 ✏️ **Listen and number.**

a

b

c

d

Can identify musical instruments

My school in the USA

   Listen and read. Then answer.

Hello. My name's Alex. Come and see my school.

1

This is my playground. How many pupils can you see?

2

My favourite lesson is music. What instruments can you see?

3

This is my teacher. Her name's Miss Ellis. What's her favourite colour?

  Look at your classroom. Ask and answer.

How many pupils can you see?

What's your teacher's name?

What's his/her favourite colour?

1 Draw your school.
2 Draw your classmates and your teacher.
3 Make a poster.

Show your poster to your family.

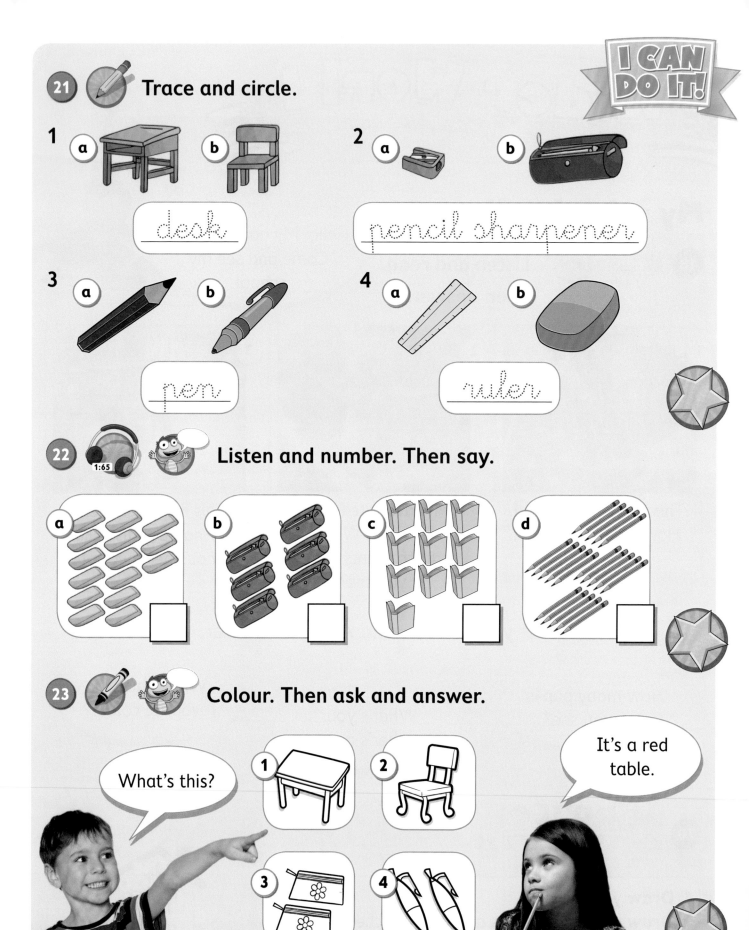

21 Trace and circle.

1 a b

desk

2 a b

pencil sharpener

3 a b

pen

4 a b

ruler

22 1:65 Listen and number. Then say.

a   b   c   d

23 Colour. Then ask and answer.

What's this?   1   2

3   4

It's a red table.

24 **Find and circle six differences.**

25 **Say and play.**

A pink pencil case.

Picture 1.

Review Units 1 and 2

1   **Listen and colour. Then trace and match.**

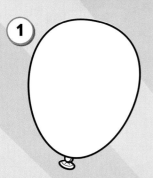 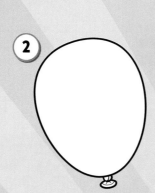 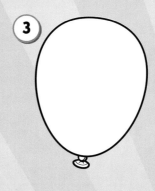 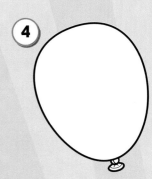

It's ___green___ . It's ___orange___ . It's ___purple___ . It's ___pink___ .

2   **Count and circle. Then say.**

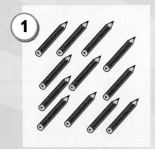 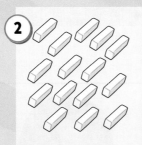  

twelve / twenty   eight / fifteen   two / three   eleven / thirteen

    Can talk about colours and numbers

 **Listen and ✓.**

1 a   b   **2** a   b

3 a   b   **4** a   b

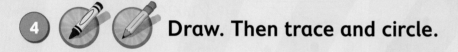 **Draw. Then trace and circle.**

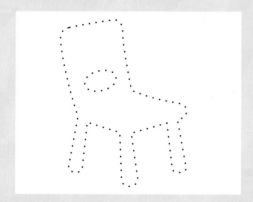

It's a (_table_ / _chain_).

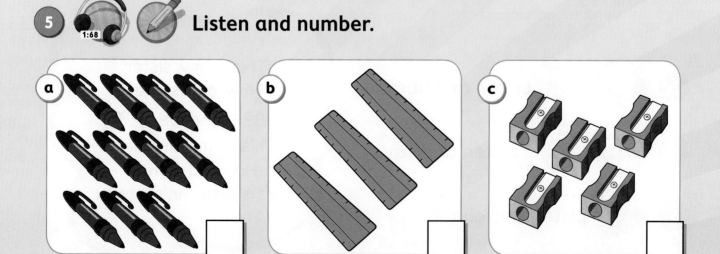 **Listen and number.**

a   b   c

3 My family

1 ⭐ **What do you know?**

2 🎧 1:69 **Listen.**

sister

brother

aunt

friend

3 🎧 1:70 ✏️ **Listen and number.**

4 🎧 1:71 💬 **Listen and say.**

5 🎧 1:72 **Listen and chant.**

This is my sister.
How old is she?
She's six, she's six!

This is my brother.
How old is he?
He's seven, he's seven!

Can identify family members

LOOK!

This is my brother/sister.

How old is he/she?	He's/She's nine.

He's = He is   She's = She is

mum   dad   granny   grandad

6 **Listen and write. Then ask and answer.**

How old is he?

He's ten.

Look for a photo today!
A balloon, a cake, a tablet and a photo!
Look for a photo today!

7 1:76 Listen and number.
Then listen again and say.

a b c d e f g h i

vet ☐ doctor ☐ cook ☐ dentist ☐ teacher ☐

pilot ☐ dancer ☐ farmer ☐ artist ☐

8 1:77 Listen, find and match. Then sing.

SONG

I'm at the airport with my family.
Brother, sister, mum and dad.
I'm glad, glad, glad.

This is my mum.
She's a pilot.
My dad is a pilot, too.

This is my sister.
She's an artist.
And my brother is a cook.

me   my dad   my sister

my brother   my mum

cut-outs

p:117

LOOK!

Is he/she a vet?	Yes, he/she is.	He's/She's a teacher.
	No, he/she isn't.	

 9  **Listen and circle. Then ask and answer.**

1  a b

2  a b

3  a
2+4=6
b

4  a b

Is she a dancer?

No, she isn't. She's an artist.

 **SKILLS**

 10 **Look and stick. Then write.**

pilot   vet   Is she   Yes   cook   No

1

Is she a teacher?

Yes , she is.

2

Is she a _____ ?

Yes, she is.

3

Is he a _____ ?

_____ , he isn't.

He's a _____ .

Stick

 Love your family.

Can understand and act out a simple story

12 **Listen.**

1 c   **2** g   **3** o

13 **Listen, point and say.**

14 **Listen and blend the sounds.**

1   c – a – n   can   2   c – a – p   cap

3   c – a – t   cat   4   g – a – s   gas

5   d – i – g   dig   6   o – n   on

7   d – o – g   dog   8   t – o – p   top

15   **Underline c, g and o. Read the words aloud.**

1 dig   **2** cap   **3** dog

4 on   **5** gas   **6** can

Listen and number. Then say.

This is my family.

a

painting

b

collage

c

sculpture

d

drawing

17   **Listen. Then ask and answer.**

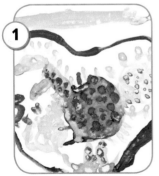 1

 2

 3

 4

Is it a painting?

Yes, it is.

Is it a dragon?

Yes, it is.

Wider World

Different families

 **18** **1:90** Listen and read.
Then match.

a

b

1

I'm Pablo and I'm 5. This is my family. My mum is a cook and her name's Maria. My dad is a vet. His name's Jorge. This is my brother Carlos. He's a baby. My sister Monica is 7.

2

I'm Tina. I'm 8. This is my family. My dad is a farmer. His name's John. My mum is an artist. Her name's Sandy. And this is my sister Carla. She's 5.

19 Read and circle.

1 Is Pablo a doctor?
Yes, he is. / No, he isn't.

2 Is Carla three?
Yes, she is. / No, she isn't.

3 How old is Pablo?
He's eight. / He's five.

4 Is Tina eight?
Yes, she is. / No, she isn't.

20 PROJECT

1 **Draw** your family.
2 **Write** about your picture.
3 **Make** a class album.

HOME SCHOOL LINK

Talk to your family about their jobs.

21 ✏️ **Trace and number.**

1 dad

2 aunt

3 granny

a ▢

b ▢

c ▢

d ▢

e ▢

f ▢

4 grandad

5 mum

6 friend

22 🎧 1:92 **Listen and number. Then say.**

a ▢

b ▢

c ▢

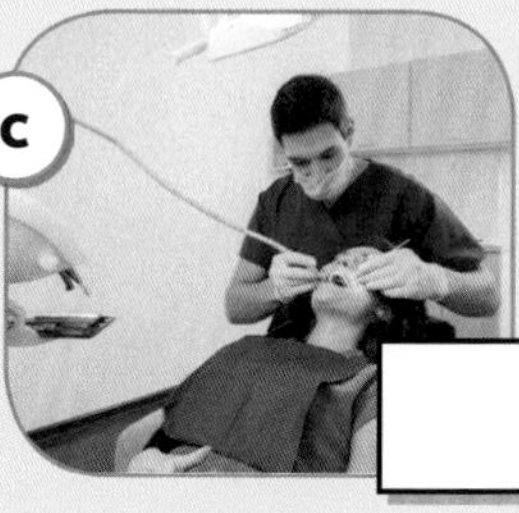

d ▢

23 **Ask and answer.**

Is he a vet?

No, he isn't.

Is he a teacher?

Yes, he is.

I CAN DO IT!

Can assess what I have learnt in Unit 3

24 **Find and circle.**

1
a
b

2
a
b

3
a
b

4
a
b

25 **Say.**

This is my mum.

She's a doctor.

4 My body

1 ⭐ **What do you know?**   **2** 🎧 2:01 **Listen.**

head

hands

arms

body

legs

feet

3 🎧 2:02 ✏️ **Listen and circle.**

4 🎧 2:03 😀💬 **Listen and say.**

5 🎧 2:04 **Listen and chant.**

I've got green arms.
I've got green hands.
I've got green legs.
I've got green feet.
I've got green wings.
I've got a green tail.
I've got a green head,
But now it's red!

Can identify parts of the body

7   Listen and number.
Then listen again and say.

a  T-shirt ☐

b  jumper ☐

c  trousers ☐

d  dress ☐

e  skirt ☐

f  shoes ☐

g  socks ☐

h  hat ☐

8   Listen and colour the clothes. Then sing.

I've got a red dress
And a blue hat.
I've got grey socks
And pink shoes.
Stamp your feet with me!
(stamp, stamp)

I've got a green T-shirt
And purple trousers.
I've got a brown jumper
And yellow shoes.
Stamp your feet with me!
(stamp, stamp)

Cut-outs

p:119

Can identify clothes

9   **Listen and stick.
Then play.**

①  ②

③  ④

 LOOK!

He's/She's got a red hat.

He's/She's got blue trousers.

He's/She's got one head.
It's yellow.

He's/She's got four legs.
They're purple.

He's got = He has got
She's got = She has got

She's got a yellow head.

Number 1!

Stick

10 **Colour. Then play.**

SKILLS

①  ②

He's got four yellow arms.

Listen and read. Then act out.

Can understand and act out a simple story

12  **Listen.**

1 **ck** **2** **e** **3** **k**

13   **Listen, point and say.**

14   **Listen and blend the sounds.**

1 k – i – ck kick   **2** s – o – ck sock

3 p – e – n pen   **4** p – e – t pet

5 t – e – n ten   **6** n – e – ck neck

7 k – i – d kid   **8** k – i – t kit

15   **Underline *ck*, *e* and *k*. Read the words aloud.**

1 pen

2 kid

3 neck

4 sock

5 kick

6 kit

16   **Listen and number. Then say.**

a

clean hands ☐

b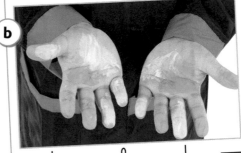

dirty hands ☐

c

a dirty face ☐

d

Wash your hands! ☐

17 **Look and circle or trace.**

1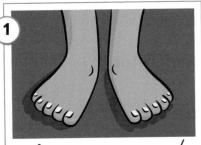

clean toes /
dirty toes

2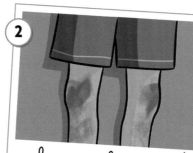

clean legs /
dirty legs

3

Wash your hands! /
Wash your face!

4

dirty neck

5

clean hands

Wider World

Carnivals in the UK

   Listen and read. Then match.

18 2:22

1
It's carnival time! There is carnival music. Look at the steel drums. How many drums can you see? What colour are they?

2
Carnival time is fun. I'm at the carnival with my friends. We've got carnival hats and I've got a pink face.

a

b

3
This is a carnival float. It's a dinosaur. It's red and black. It's got a tail and it's got a big head.

c

  Look and play.

19

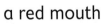 a red mouth

 Picture c.

  PROJECT

20

1 **Draw** pictures of a carnival in your country.
2 **Write** about the pictures.
3 **Make** a poster.

HOME SCHOOL LINK
Talk to your family about carnivals in your country.

21 Trace and match.

1 head

2 hands

3 legs

4 feet

5 arms

6 toes

7 body

8 fingers

22 2:23 Write. Then listen and ✓ or ✗.

I've got _____ feet.

1 ☐   2 ☐

3 ☐   4 ☐

5 ☐   6 ☐

23 Look. Ask and answer.

I've got three heads.

No.

I've got a purple body.

Yes!

24   **Find and circle two the same. Then say.**

1

2

3

I've got four legs.

25   **Draw and colour. Then play.**

I've got green legs.

I've got four arms. They're orange.

Units 3 and 4

1 **Listen and number.**

 a

 b

 c

 d

 e

 f

2 **Listen and ✓. Then ask and answer.**

1  a   b

2  a   b

3  a   b

4  a   b

Is she a pilot?

No, she isn't.
She's a vet.

Can talk about family members and occupations

3 ✏️ **Look and trace. Then write.**

1 head
2 arm
3 hand
4 fingers
5 leg
6 body
7 foot

vet   dentist   dancer

She's a _____.

4 🎧 **2:26** ✏️ **Listen and draw.**

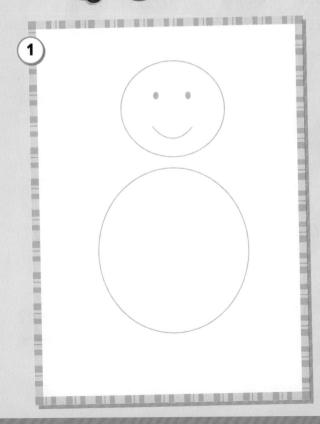

1

2

5 Pets

1 ⭐ **What do you know?**

2 🎧 2:27 **Listen.**

mouse

hamster

dog cat

rabbit

3 🎧 2:28 ✏️ **Listen and circle.**

4 🎧 2:29 💬 **Listen and say.**

5 🎧 2:30 **Listen and chant.**

Pets, pets.
Big and small!
Come and listen
to them all.

What's that?
It's a parrot.
A parrot!

What are those?
They're snakes.
Snakes!

What's that?
It's a dog.
A dog!

What are those?
They're hamsters.
Hamsters!

parrot

snake

tortoise

frog

LOOK! 2:31

| What's **that**? | **It's a** dog. |
| What are **those**? | **They're** hamsters. |

TIP!
one mouse /
two mice

6 2:32 **Listen and number. Then ask and answer.**

a   b   c   d   e `1`   f   g   h

What's that?   It's a cat.

What are those?   They're rabbits.

Quest 2:33
Look for a bird today.
A balloon, a cake, a tablet,
a photo, a teddy and a bird!
Look for a bird today!

7 2:34 Listen and number.
Then listen again and say.

a   b   c   d   e

big ☐   small ☐   tall ☐   short ☐   long ☐

f   g   h   i

thin ☐   fat ☐   young ☐   old ☐

8 2:35 Listen and circle. Then sing.

SONG

TIP!
very **big** /
very **small**

The boy's got a dog
A very /  .
He's got a dog. Woof! Woof!

The dog's got a frog
A very  / .
The dog's got a frog. Ribbit! Ribbit!

The girl's got a cat
A very / 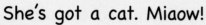 .
She's got a cat. Miaow!

The cat's got a hat
A very / .
The cat's got a hat. Miaow!

He's got a dog.

The dog's got a frog.

She's got a cat,

And the cat's got a hat!

p:121

LOOK!

		Yes, I **have**. **It's a** small parrot.
Have you **got**	a parrot?	No, I **haven't**.
Has he/she **got**		Yes, he/she **has**. **It's a** small parrot.
		No, he/she **hasn't**. **He's/She's got** a big dog.

haven't = have not   hasn't = has not

9 **Listen and write ✓ or ✗. Then ask and answer.**

1  **2**  **3**  **4**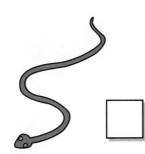

> Have you got a parrot?

> Yes, I have. It's a fat parrot.

10 **Listen and stick. Then play.**

 SKILLS

1  **2**  **3**  **4**

> Has he got a thin cat?

> No, he hasn't. He's got a fat hamster.

> Number 1?

> Correct!

 Stick

Listen and read. Then act out.

 Take care of your pets.

Can understand and act out a simple story

12 **Listen.**
2:42

1 **b**   **2** **h**   **3** **r**   **4** **u**

13   **Listen, point and say.**
2:43

14   **Listen and blend the sounds.**
2:44

1 | b – a – g | bag   **2** | r – u – g | rug

3 | h – o – t | hot   **4** | h – a – t | hat

5 | r – e – d | red   **6** | r – a – t | rat

7 | u – p | up   **8** | c – u – p | cup

15   **Underline *b*, *h*, *r* and *u*. Read the words aloud.**

1   rat   **2**   cup   **3**   rug

4   hat   **5**   red   **6**   bag

16   2:48 **Listen and point. Then match and say.**

1

cat

2

dog

3

bird

a

chick

b

kitten

c

puppy

17 2:49 **Listen and number. Then say.**

a

goose

b

egg

c

chick

It's an egg.

Wider World

Unusual pets

18  2:50 **Listen and read. Then circle.**

1  My name's Angela. I've got a small pet. It's brown and it's got four legs. It's got a long tail. It's a (spider / rat).

2  My name's Ben. My pet is small and green. It's a got four legs and a tail. It's a (lizard / snake).

3  My name's Grace. I've got a small pet. It's black and it's got eight legs. It's a (spider / lizard).

 spider

 lizard

 rat

19   **Ask and answer. Write ✓ or ✗.**

Have you got a spider?

No, I haven't.

20  **PROJECT**

1 Draw an unusual pet.
2 Write about your picture.
3 Make a poster.

 HOME SCHOOL LINK

Ask your family to help you find pictures of unusual pets.

21 Read and match.

 1
 2
 3
 4
 5
 6

b parrot

d hamster

f tortoise

a cat

c rabbit

e dog

22 Listen and number. Then say.

 a

 b

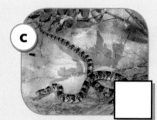 c

What's that?

 d

 e

 f

It's a fat cat.

23 Ask and answer.

Have you got a cat?

No, I haven't.

Have you got a hamster?

Yes, I have.

24   **Play.**

25 **2:52** **Listen and do.**

6 My house

1 ⭐ What do you know?

2 🎧 2:53 Listen.

bedroom ☐

garden ☐

living room ☐

house ☐

door ☐

3  🎧 2:54 Listen and number.

4  🎧 2:55 Listen and say.

5  🎧 2:56 Listen and chant.

Where's my mum?
She's in the living room. (x2)

Where's my dad?
He's in the kitchen. (x2)

Where's Harry?
He's in the bathroom. (x2)

Where are Waldo and Beth?
They're in the bedroom. (x2)

Can identify rooms and parts of my house

window ☐

bathroom ☐

🎧 2:57 **LOOK!**

Where's Aunt Fifi?	She's in the living room.
Where are Waldo and Beth?	They're in the bedroom.

Where's = Where is

kitchen ☐

Quest 🔍 2:59

Look for a door today.
A balloon, a cake, a tablet, a photo, a teddy, a bird and a door!
Look for a door today!

6 🎧 2:58 💬 **Listen and ✓ or X. Then ask and answer.**

 1 ☐

 2 ☐

 3 ☐

 4 ☐

Where's Waldo?

He's in the bathroom.

7   **Listen and point.**
Then listen again and say.

1. bed

2. cooker

3. fridge

4. TV

5. sofa

6. lamp

7. bath

8. sink

8   **Listen and circle. Then sing.**

SONG

Where's the mouse?
Where's the mouse?

Is it in the garden?
Or is it in the house?

Look! It's in the garden.
Running up the path.

Now it's in the /  .

Oh no! It's in the / 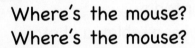 !

Where's the mouse?
Where's the mouse?

Is it in the garden?
Or is it in the house?

Look! It's in the garden.
Hiding in the shed.

Now it's in the 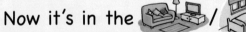 / .

Oh no! It's in my / !

Cut-outs
p:123

9   **Listen and ✓.
Then say.**

 **LOOK!**

There's a lamp on the desk.

There are two kittens under the sofa.

There's = There is

1

2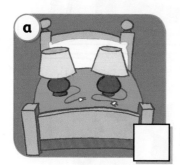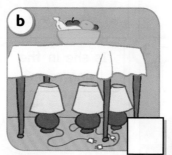

TIP!

under

on

in

There's a TV
on the cooker.

10 **Listen and stick. Then play.**

 **SKILLS**

 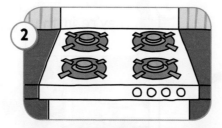 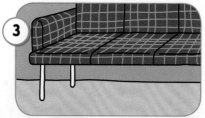

There are two books on the table.

Number 6. My turn.

Stick

Listen and read. Then act out.

VALUES Be tidy.

12 **Listen.**

1 f **2**  ff **3** l **4** ll

13  **Listen, point and say.**

14  **Listen and blend the sounds.**

1 f – i – g fig **2** f – a – n fan

3 o – ff off **4** p – u – ff puff

5 l – e – g leg **6** l – a – p lap

7 d – o – ll doll **8** b – e – ll bell

15   **Underline f, ff, l and ll. Read the words aloud.**

1 leg **2** doll **3** fig

4 puff **5** bell **6** fan

16 Listen and number. Then say.

SOCIAL SCIENCE

a shop ☐

b library ☐

c playground ☐

d park ☐

e café ☐

17 Listen and match. Then say.

1

3

2

a

b

c

She's in the playground.

Can talk about places in the neighbourhood

Wider World

Different homes

   Listen and read. Then match.

1 My name's Ravi. I live on a houseboat. It's a big boat. There's a living room and two bedrooms. My favourite room is the living room.

a

2 My name's Rosie. I live in a caravan! It's small but it's nice. There's a living room, a kitchen and a bathroom.

b

3 My name's Juan. I live in a big flat. There's a kitchen, a living room, two bathrooms and four bedrooms. I've got a TV in my bedroom.

c

  Ask and answer.

Where do you live?

Do you live in a house?

  PROJECT

1 **Draw** your home.
2 **Write** about your picture.
3 **Make** a class display.

HOME SCHOOL LINK

Talk about your home with your family.

21 Look and write.

1   **2**   **3**

living room _____ _____

4  **5**

_____ _____

22 Look and ✓. Then say.

There's a sink in the kitchen.

23 Talk about your house.

In my house, there are three bedrooms.

In my house, there's a TV in the kitchen.

Can assess what I have learnt in Unit 6

24   **Find and circle. Then ask and answer.**

Where's Beth?

She's in the library.

Review Units 5 and 6

1 2:80   **Listen and ✓ or ✗.**

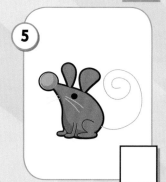   

2 **Look and write.**

~~big~~	long		dog	~~rabbit~~
small	young		snake	tortoise

1 She's got a
big
rabbit.

2 He's got a
_____
_____.

3 She's got a
_____
_____.

4 He's got a
_____
_____.

Can talk about pets

Listen and match. Then ask and answer.

1

2

3

4

a

b

c

d

4  **Listen and draw.**

7 Food

1 ⭐ **What do you know?** **2** 🎧 3:01 **Listen.**

salad

fruit

cake

bread

juice

3 🎧 3:02 ✏️ **Listen and circle.**

4 🎧 3:03 😀 **Listen and say.**

I like fruit and yoghurt.
I don't like fish and cheese.
I like cake and milk and salad.
Can I have some, please?

5 🎧 3:04 **Listen and chant.**

Can identify food items

LOOK!

3:05

I **like** cake and milk.
I **don't like** salad and fish.

yoghurt

cheese

milk

fish

6 3:06 **Listen and match. Then ask and answer.**

I like fish.

You're Waldo.

Quest

3:07

Look for an apple today.
A balloon, a cake, a tablet,
a photo, a teddy, a bird,
a door and an apple!
Look for an apple today!

7   **Listen and stick. Then listen again and say.**

1  **2** **3** **4**

sandwich   water   chocolate   honey

5 **6** **7** **8**

jelly   vegetables   ice cream   meat

8   **Listen and circle. Then sing.**

I like / . It's nice and sweet!

I like / . It's good to eat!

I like / . But I don't like / .

I like / . But I don't like bees!

Yes, I like honey. But I don't like bees. (x3)

p:125

9 **3:12** **Listen and write ✓ or ✗.**
Then ask and answer.

3:11 Do you like honey?	Yes, I do.
	No, I don't.

	 HONEY	salad	fruit	yogurt	cake	WATER
Ellie	✓					
Me						
My friend						

Do you like honey? Yes, I do. Me too!

10 **3:13** **Listen and guess.**

SKILLS

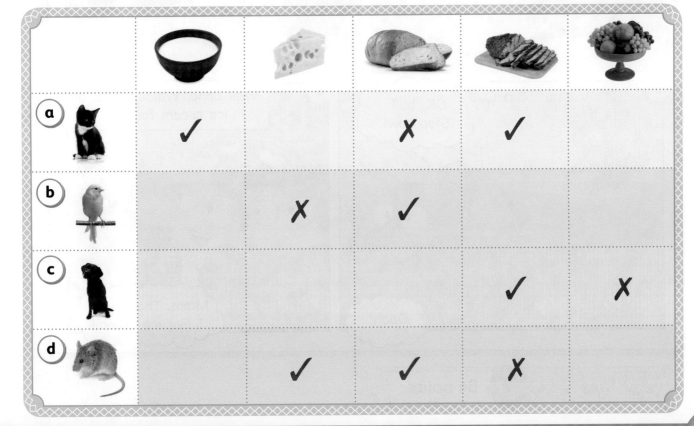

		milk	cheese	bread	meat	fruit
a	cat	✓		✗	✓	
b	bird		✗	✓		
c	dog				✓	✗
d	mouse		✓	✓	✗	

Lesson 4   Can ask and answer questions about food using *Do you like...?*   **81**

Listen and read. Then act out.

Can understand and act out a simple story

12  3:17 **Listen.**

1 **j** **2** **ss** **3** **v** **4** **w**

13 3:18 **Listen, point and say.**

14  3:19 **Listen and blend the sounds.**

1 j – a – m jam   **2** j – e – t jet

3 k – i – ss kiss   **4** m – e – ss mess

5 v – a – n van   **6** v – e – t vet

7 w – e – b web   **8** w – i – g wig

15   **Underline *j*, *ss*, *v* and *w*. Read the words aloud.**

1 jet   **2** wig   **3** kiss

4 web   **5** van   **6** jam

Listen and number. Then say.

a

sausages

b

carrots

c

chips

 Look and ✓ the foods that are good for you. Then say.

I like salad. It's good for me.

I like chocolate. It's bad for me.

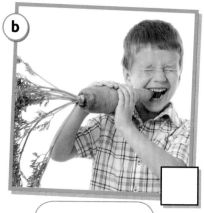

1

2

3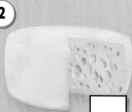

4

5

6

7

8

Can talk about foods that are good and bad for me

Wider World

Packed lunches

18 3:24 **Listen and read. Then match.**

a

1 I've got sandwiches and fruit. I've got a yoghurt. I like yoghurt but I don't like jelly. I like milk but I don't like juice.

b

2 I've got bread and cheese and salad. I like salad but I don't like fruit. I like chocolate. I like juice but I don't like milk.

c

3 I've got chicken and vegetables. I don't like bread. I like juice and I like chocolate. I don't like milk and I don't like yoghurt.

19 **Ask and answer.**

Have you got a packed lunch?

What do you like for lunch?

Do you like sandwiches?

20 **PROJECT**

1 **Draw** your favourite packed lunch.
2 **Write** about your picture.
3 **Talk** about your picture with your classmates.

 **HOME SCHOOL LINK**

Talk about your lunch with your family. Is it good for you?

21 **Look and write.**

①  ②  ③  ④  ⑤

 bread _____ _____ _____ _____

⑥  ⑦  ⑧  ⑨  ⑩

_____ _____ _____ _____ _____

22 **Draw and write. Then say.**

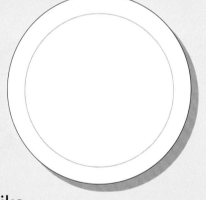

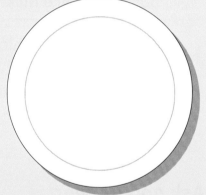

I like _____
and _____ .

I don't like _____
and _____ .

23 **Ask and answer.**

Do you like fish?

Yes, I do. It's good for me.

24 Find and draw ☺ or ☹.
Then ask and answer.

I like chocolate.

You're Harry.

Lesson 10

Can use what I have learnt in Unit 7

8 I'm happy!

1 ⭐ **What do you know?**

2 🎧 3:27 **Listen.**

tired

hungry

thirsty

scared

happy

3 🎧 3:28 ✏️ **Listen and number.**

4 🎧 3:29 💬 **Listen and say.**

5 🎧 3:30 **Listen and chant.**

Are you tired, tired, tired?
Are you tired?
No, I'm not.

Are you hungry, hungry, hungry?
Are you hungry?
No, I'm not.

Are you scared, scared, scared?
Are you scared?
No, I'm not.

Are you thirsty, thirsty, thirsty?
Are you thirsty?
No, I'm not.

Are you happy, happy, happy?
Are you happy?
Yes, I am!

Can identify feelings

Are you hungry? | Yes, **I am.**
No, **I'm not.**

6 3:32 **Listen and match. Then ask and answer.**

a   b   c   d   e

1   2   3   4   5

Are you scared?

Yes, I am.

You're Waldo.

Quest 3:33
Look for a hat today.
A balloon, a cake, a tablet,
a photo, a teddy, a bird,
a door, an apple and a hat!
Look for a hat today!

7 **3:35** Listen and act.
Then listen again and say.

1 sad

2 cold

3 hot

4 ill

5 hurt

6 angry

7 bored

8 **3:36** Listen and circle. Then sing and act out.

SONG

5, 4, 3, 2, 1.
I'm (hot / cold)
And (sad / happy).
Let's have fun!

Clap your hands.
Stamp your feet.
Click your fingers.
Drink and eat.

6, 7, 8, 9, 10.
I'm (hurt / cold)
And sick.
I'm going to bed!

Wiggle your toes.
Let's all lie down.
Roll over once.
Now turn around.

5, 4, 3, 2, 1.
I'm (angry / tired)
And (bored / scared).
Good night to you!

cutouts

p:127

Listen and stick. Then circle.

1

bored / scared

2

hot / cold

3

happy / sad

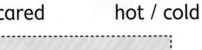 **LOOK!**

Is he/she cold?	Yes, **he/she is.**
	No, **he/she isn't.** **He's/She's** hurt.
Are they bored?	Yes, **they are.**
	No, **they aren't.** **They're** tired.
aren't = are not	

Stick

10 **Ask and answer.**

SKILLS

1

2

3

4

5

6

Are they thirsty?

Are they hurt?

Number 6!

No, they aren't.

Yes, they are.

VALUES Respect feelings. Help others.

12 3:42 **Listen.**

1 **qu** **2** **x** **3** **y** **4** **z** **5** **zz**

13 3:43 **Listen, point and say.**

14 3:44 **Listen and blend the sounds.**

1 qu – i – z   quiz   2 qu – i – ck   quick

3 b – o – x   box   4 t – a – x – i   taxi

5 y – e – s   yes   6 y – e – ll   yell

7 z – a – p   zap   8 z – i – p   zip

9 b – u – zz   buzz   10 f – i – zz   fizz

15   **Underline *qu*, *x*, *y*, *z* and *zz*. Read the words aloud.**

1 zip

2 taxi

3 buzz

4 yes

5 quiz

6 box

Listen and say. Then circle.

hot cold

SOCIAL SCIENCE

1

2

3

It's (hot / cold).   It's (hot / cold).   It's (hot / cold).

   Listen and match. Then say.

1   **2**   **3**   **4**

penguin   snake   polar bear   turtle

a

b

c

d

It's a snake.   It's hot.

Can identify animals that live where it's hot and cold

Wider World

Hot and cold places in the USA

18  **Listen and read. Then match.**

1 I'm Fay. I live in Alaska. It's cold here. I've got a hat.

2 I'm Sam. I live in Florida. It's hot here. I like the sea.

3 This is my house in Florida. I like my house.

4 This is my house in Alaska. I like snow!

a

b

c

d

19 **Read and circle.**

1 (Florida / Alaska) is cold.

2 (Florida / Alaska) is hot.

3 Sam likes the (sea / snow).

4 Fay likes the (sea / snow).

20

1 **Draw** where you live.
2 **Write** about your picture.
3 **Make** a poster with your classmates.

HOME SCHOOL LINK
Talk about your home with your family. Is it hot or cold?

21 Look and write.

1. I'm *happy*.

2. I'm _____.

3. I'm _____.

4. I'm _____.

22 3:51 Listen and number. Then write.

a □ He's *thirsty*.

b □ She's _____.

c □ She's _____.

d □ He's _____.

23 Ask and answer.

Are you ill?

No, I'm not.

Are you happy?

Yes, I am.

Can assess what I have learnt in Unit 8

24   **Find and match.**
Then ask and answer.

1
2
3
4

5
6
7
8

Is he scared?

Yes, he is.

Number 1.

   1 Listen and draw ☺ or ☹.

Max

Anna

2 Read and number.

 a

 b

 c

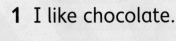 **1** I like chocolate.

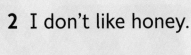 **2** I don't like honey.

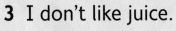 **3** I don't like juice.

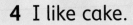 **4** I like cake.

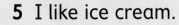 **5** I like ice cream.

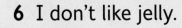 **6** I don't like jelly.

 d

 e

 f

Can talk about food and dislikes

3 **Listen and ✓. Then ask and answer.**

1  a ☐ b ☐

2  a ☐ b ☐

3  a ☐ b ☐

4   a ☐ b ☐

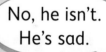
Is he scared?

No, he isn't.
He's sad.

4 **Look and write.**

1 She's ___cold___.　　**2** He's _____.　　**3** She's _____.　　**4** He's _____.

Goodbye

1 3:54 🎧 ✏️ **Listen, find and circle.**

2 3:55 🎧 ✏️ **Listen and number.**

a ⬜
b ⬜
c ⬜
d ⬜
e ⬜

f ⬜
g ⬜
h ⬜
i ⬜

Can identify the Quest items

3 Count and write. Then ask and answer.

There are [ ] Quest items.

| balloon tablet apple cake door |
| teddy photo bird hat |

a _____   b _____   c _____

d _____   e _____   f _____

g _____   h _____   i _____

There's a bird.   Yes!

Find and circle six differences. Then listen and check.

In picture 1, he's happy.

In picture 2, he's sad.

5 **Look at picture 2. Read and match.**

1 Has she got blue shoes?

2 How many sandwiches can you see?

3 Is he happy?

4 Where's the frog?

5 Has he got a parrot?

a It's on the chair.

b No, he hasn't.

c Yes, she has.

d Four.

e No, he isn't.

Can use what I have learnt in Level 1

6 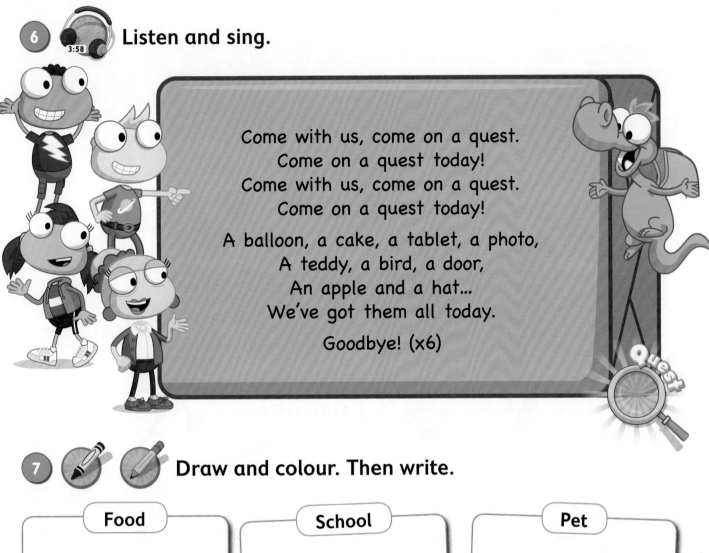 Listen and sing.

Come with us, come on a quest.
Come on a quest today!
Come with us, come on a quest.
Come on a quest today!

A balloon, a cake, a tablet, a photo,
A teddy, a bird, a door,
An apple and a hat...
We've got them all today.

Goodbye! (x6)

7  Draw and colour. Then write.

Food

School

Pet

8 Show a friend. Ask and answer.

Is it a parrot?   Yes, it is.

Halloween

1  **Listen, find and say.**

monster

witch

cat

pumpkin

bat

2  **Listen and sing.**

3  **Make a pumpkin and play.**

It's Halloween, it's Halloween,
Pass the pumpkin, 1, 2, 3.
Pass the pumpkin to me!

I'm a monster. I'm a bat.
I'm a pumpkin. I'm a witch, ha, ha, ha!
And I've got a cat.

It's Halloween, it's Halloween,
Pass the pumpkin, 1, 2, 3.
Pass the pumpkin to me!

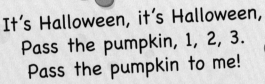

Can sing a song about Halloween

Christmas

1  **Listen, find and say.**

Santa

present

reindeer

sleigh

2  **Listen and sing.**

3 **Make a Christmas card for your family.**

It's Christmas Day (x2),
Here comes Santa in his sleigh!
It's Christmas Day (x2),
Santa's on his way.

Look at the reindeer, 1, 2, 3.
Look at the presents. Can you see?
Red, yellow, green and blue,
Orange, pink and purple, too!

It's Christmas Day...
Happy Christmas!

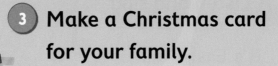

Easter

1  **Listen, find and say.**

chick

egg

bunny

2 **Listen and sing.**

It's Easter time,
Time for fun.

Can you see the chicks
Go cheep, cheep, cheep?
Can you see the bunny
Go hop, hop, hop?
Can you see the eggs
For you and me, you and me?

Find, find, find, find the chicks,
Find, find, find, find the bunny,
Find, find, find, find the eggs.

It's Easter time,
Time for fun
Happy Easter everyone!

3 **Make an Easter egg.**
Have an egg hunt.

Can sing a song about Easter

Summer fun

1  **Listen, find and say.**

sky · bird · tree · sun · flower · grass

2  **Listen and chant.**

3 **Make and play.**

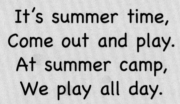

It's summer time,
Come out and play.
At summer camp,
We play all day.

The grass is green,
The trees are, too.
The flowers are red,
And the sky is blue.

It's summer time...

The birds are happy.
They sing in the sun.
And we are happy.
Summer camp is fun!

Grammar Reference

Welcome

Names and identifying characters:

Hello. My name's Harry.

I'm Harry.

His name's Harry.

His balloon is red.

Goodbye.

Her name's Beth.

Her balloon is blue.

name's = name is

Imperatives:

Stand up! Sit down!

Unit 1

Personal questions:

What's your name?

How old are you?

What's your favourite colour?

What's = What is

My name's Cody.

I'm seven.

My favourite colour is green.

I'm = I am

Asking about colours (singular objects):

Is it purple?

What colour is it?

It's = It is

Yes, it is./No, it isn't.

It's pink.

Isn't = Is not

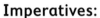

Unit 2

Identifying objects (singular and plural):

What's this?	It's a book. It's red. It's a red book.
What are these?	They're pencils.
	They're = They are

Asking about colours (plural objects):

What colour are they?	They're red.
How many pencils can you see?	Five.

Unit 3

Introducing family members:

This is my brother/sister.

Asking and answering about age:

How old is he/she?	He's/She's nine.
	He's/She's = He is/She is

Asking and answering about occupations:

Is he/she a dancer?	Yes, he/she is.
Is he/she an artist?	No, he/she isn't. He's/She's a cook.

Unit 4

Talking about possession:

I've got a green tail.	I've got green arms.
He's got blue trousers.	She's got a yellow head.
She's got four legs. They're purple.	
I've got = I have got	He's/She's got = He/She has got

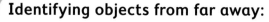

Unit 5

Identifying objects from far away:

What's that?   It's a dog.

What are those?   They're hamsters.

Asking and answering about possession:

Have you got a parrot?   Yes, I have. It's a small parrot.

                              No, I haven't.

Has he/she got a parrot?   Yes, she has. It's a small parrot.

                              No, he hasn't. He's got a big dog.

haven't = have not   hasn't = has not

Unit 6

Asking and answering about location:

Where's Aunt Fifi?   She's in the living room.

Where are Waldo and Beth?   They're in the bedroom.

Where's = Where is

Describing a room:

There's a lamp on the desk.   There are two kittens under the sofa.

There's = There is

Unit 7

Expressing likes and dislikes with food:

I like cake and milk.

I don't like salad and fish.

don't = do not

Asking and answering about likes and dislikes:

Do you like honey?

Yes, I do./No, I don't.

Unit 8

Expressing emotion:

I'm hungry.

He's/She's thirsty.

Asking and answering about feelings:

Are you hungry?

Yes, I am./No, I'm not.

Is he/she cold?

Yes, he is.

No, she isn't. She's hurt.

Are they bored?

Yes, they are.

No, they aren't. They're tired.

aren't = are not

 **What can you do in English? Ask and say. Then ✓.**

Can you say your name? ☐

Can you say your age? ☐

Can you name six colours? ☐

Can you say your favourite colour? ☐

Can you say four action words? ☐

Can you name five school objects? ☐

Can you count to twenty? ☐

Can you describe your family? ☐

Can you name five jobs? ☐

Can you name six parts of the body? ☐

Can you name five items of clothing? ☐

Can you name the rooms in a house? ☐

Can you describe the furniture in your bedroom? ☐

Can you name seven animals? ☐

Can you describe animals? ☐

Can you say the food you like? ☐

Can you say the food you don't like? ☐

Can you name two food items that are bad for you? ☐

Can you say how you are feeling today? ☐

Cut and play, Unit 1, page 14.

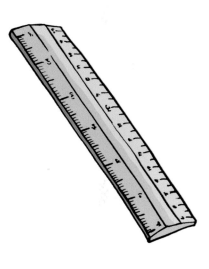

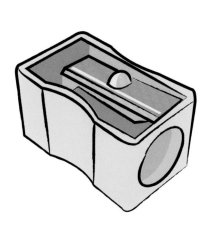

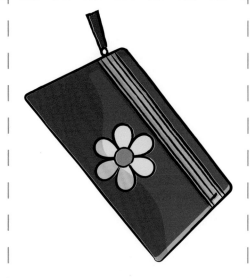

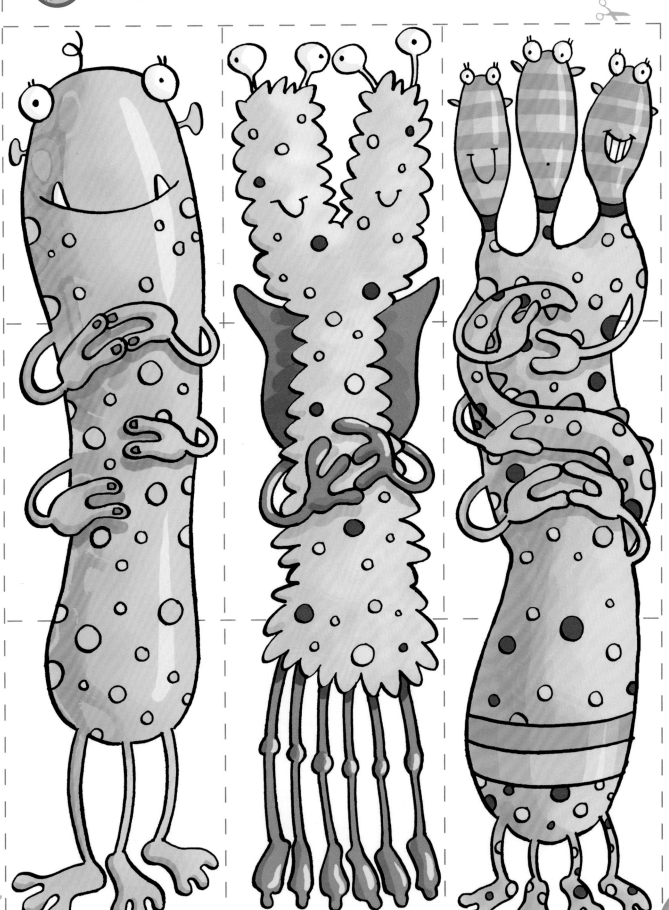

Cut and play, Unit 5, page 58.

Cut and play, Unit 6, page 68.

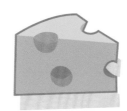

Yoghurt

HONEY